Courageous Gratitude

Celebrate Your Journey through Motherhood

By Deborah Woods, National Certified Counselor

PLAYTIME BAY PUBLISHING

This book is the first in the Playtime Presence Series.

For more information on the next book in this series, <u>Brave Empathy: A Feelings Field Guide</u>, you can contact the author, Deborah Woods, NCC at her email address Deborah@deborahwoodsncc.com

If you are interested in using some of what I wrote or to make it available in some way, please contact me so we can explore that. I can be contacted at: Deborah@deborahwoodsncc.com

Protecting copyright is a powerful way to show your support while acknowledging in gratitude the work that took months to complete and ensuring that it can be made available. Thank you!

I hope this book encourages you to reflect, to imagine and dream about the possible relationships you could have with your children. I hope it inspires you to see in your mind's eye the relationships you'd like your children to have with their children. I hope it minimizes the mistakes made, casts off the burden of perfection, and inspires gentleness and forgiveness. I hope this book inspires you to see new possibilities in yourself and in your children.

This book is educational information only. It's not advice. No therapeutic advice is being given and no therapist/patient, or counselor/client relationship is created.

Please join me on this journey. Discover the delights of courageous gratitude.

Dedication

This book is dedicated to the children who have taught me to play, to connect, and to enjoy life with a grateful heart, during times of blue skies and butterflies, epic bubble battles, and during the storms of life. Chief among these teachers has been my amazing son, Ryan. I am grateful for our adventures together. You are the sunshine that warms my heart. May the autumn leaves always fall joyfully for you.

Grab your courage. Bring your gentleness and plan to use it generously.

Come join me on a great adventure to explore the depths and heights of your gratitude as a mother. Discover the refreshing joy that awaits you around the bend and over the next ridge.

You'll find some unexpected reserves of forgiveness and grace along the way, tucked here and there. You'll need those, both for yourself and for others. Don't be afraid to use them freely. I've discovered forgiveness and grace to have some wonderful healing qualities that will help you, not only to continue, but to also enjoy the journey along the way.

Best of all, when you get to the end, you'll be pleased you took this leap of faith. You will find your way. You'll discover that you're not alone. You walk a road many have walked before you, although you're the only one who'll ever walk this exact path exactly the way you are. You are unique. And you're not alone.

I've been on this path for a while now and I can tell you it's been quite the journey. I'm so glad our paths have crossed.

Before we dive in, I want you to know …

I hate it when I'm hurting, and someone says, "You just need to be grateful. You should count your blessings."

It reminds me of when my stepmother used to ignore my objections by saying, "You know, there are kids in China who are starving. You should be grateful for what you have."

Somehow, it never helped me feel any more satisfied or comfortable with my circumstances. I always wanted to tell her to just send what I didn't want to those kids in China. Maybe they'd like it because I sure didn't.

I discovered you can't shame someone into feeling grateful.

Some people want us to "be grateful" so we won't complain. Complainers can be tough to tolerate. It's hard to stay connected with someone when they're distressed by an uncomfortable emotion that prompts them to complain.

I don't blame my stepmother. She didn't have anyone giving her empathy and encouragement. She couldn't give what she didn't have. She was truly doing the best she knew how to do. I get it. It makes sense to me that her advice to just be grateful, was designed to shut me down, to stop my whining.

The trouble is, when we put up and shut up because others don't want to hear our complaints, we aren't really feeling a sense of gratitude. We keep our feelings to ourselves because we get that others don't want to hear our thoughts, feelings, objections, and preferences.

When we're struggling, that's exactly when we need empathy and a comforting presence.

I want you to know, at the start of this journey, that this book is not about that kind of "just be grateful" experience.

I believe that gratitude can only be felt and experienced when we acknowledge the struggle and look deep inside it for the hidden treasures, the lessons, the decisions we can make to change things.

Gratitude isn't easy or cheap. It costs us something.

Courageous gratitude necessitates being willing to do some exploration, sometimes into dark and murky places we'd rather not visit. It means being willing to look for things we missed the first time around. While there are exciting discoveries and sweet experiences to be savored along the way, it often means a bit of discomfort here and there. Those who travel this road do it because we get all this wonderful joy in the end.

It's a journey for the bravest of travelers. It's not for tourists looking for a delightful rest at a holiday resort. It's not for the carefree wanderers without direction or purpose. Sightseers may not enjoy all the sights.

And still, the journey is worth the venture. Gratitude, a truly grateful heart, is worth the hike.

Purposefully noticing and writing down the good things in our lives, directs our focus and trains our minds. Soon, we discover we're seeing and remembering more of the sunny things in life. After a while, finding good things to appreciate becomes a natural part of our journey. Because we've expanded our capacity to notice and remember those things for which we can be grateful, the walk is more pleasant.

The mothering part of my journey began when I was waiting for the birth of my son. I felt confident that I knew how to be a good mom. In college I'd studied child psychology and child development. I felt prepared to raise a child. I was sure my child would be happy and well adjusted.

UNTIL my son was born. Suddenly, I discovered being a mom was much harder than I ever thought possible. I wasn't prepared for what I was up against as a mom.

The challenges my husband and I faced raising our son stressed our marriage nearly to the breaking point. I spent more time crying and wondering what was wrong with me than taking pictures of my precious little boy. My husband took this photo of us together.

Today, I'm proud of the man my son has grown into. He's overcome learning disabilities and anxiety. He's developed great people skills. He's well liked and successful at work. He's happily married and celebrating a wedding anniversary soon. We all have a close and loving relationship. He seeks my advice when he needs it. He's strong and independent and capable. I'm proud of how I raised him. Instead of crying myself to sleep these days, I cry tears of joy remembering how far we've come.

Hi, I'm Deborah Woods, National Certified Counselor. What lights me up is knowing that the things my son, my husband, and I struggled with has enabled me to help so many other moms, dads, grandparents, and kids avoid the years of pain and frustration we suffered.

This journal will bring you a refreshing new perspective on the great adventure that is motherhood. Because being a mother can be hard, it's easy to overlook the sweet moments of pleasure. As you begin to feel the swell of gratitude in your heart, you will be renewed. You'll discover memories to treasure that energize you in the valleys and on the mountain tops. You'll find happiness in the nuggets you tuck into your heart.

Join me on this personal journey as you explore your own childhood, your experience of your parents, and your thoughts about the things you brought with you, from your childhood, into your life as a mom. Our thoughts and feelings about the things we experienced as a child influence how we show up as a mom and how we do motherhood. You'll look at your thoughts and feelings about your child as you notice things you enjoy about your child. You'll explore the things you are proud of in the way you're being a mom. You may become aware of some ways you'd like to see your child grow through some challenges. You may become aware of some ways you'd like to grow. I wouldn't be surprised if you discovered that you've already grown in lovely ways since becoming a mother.

This journey is for you. Take it as fast or slow as you want to take it. There's no need to rush or push yourself too hard. The growth is waiting for you when you're ready. Just don't wait too long or you'll find the kids growing faster than you do. There were so many lessons that I wish I'd learned earlier. Take advantage of my mistakes. Avoid some of them entirely.

Taking the time to focus on yourself as a mom will enable you to give your child the benefit of your discoveries. The pages are designed to take you through a 40-day journey, one writing prompt a day. I've given you a space to record the date you do each prompt. You decide how many you do and how often you do them. It's up to you. The important part is that you get started. Notice if you're beginning to feel overwhelmed. That's a good time to take a break and come back fresh another day.

Stop in at my Facebook group: *Play Connect Influence*. Ask a question. Post a comment about what you're noticing. I'd love to hear about your experiences and support you in the group.
You'll find the Facebook group at: https://www.facebook.com/groups/playconnect/

Day 1: _____

Because our thoughts and feelings about motherhood began in our own childhoods, start by remembering what it was like to be a child.

If I could relive one moment of my childhood, it would be when ...

Day 2: _____

No mother's perfect. You may have had a mom who came close to perfect, or perhaps your mother was deeply challenged by things that hindered her ability to love and care for her children the way she would have liked.

Either way, it's helpful to explore how your mother's strengths and vulnerabilities impacted your life.

I wish my mother had been more ...

Day 3: _____

I wish my mother had been less ...

Day 4: _____

I am glad my mother was ...

If you're like me and survived your childhood with a whole host of bad memories, some of these questions may be painful.

I was once publicly asked to speak for 2 minutes about the life lessons I learned from my parents. I went blank. I couldn't think of a single cute, sweet, or inspirational life lesson to amuse and entertain my audience. Instead, my mind was flooded with a whole barrage of painful images, none of which I thought the audience would want to hear.

Later, when I got home, I sat at my typewriter and allowed myself to brainstorm about the lessons I learned, many of which I learned from the things my parents didn't do that I wished they would have, or from the mistakes they didn't know they were making. Not all lessons are learned from happy memories. Allow yourself to explore even the uncomfortable memories and the feelings that come with them. Surprisingly, some better memories emerged in the days that followed.

Eventually, I remembered how my stepmother made doll clothes for my dolls and I found myself feeling grateful. Then, I was in my playroom and I noticed a plaid shirt she'd made for my son's Cabbage Patch doll who came with an astronaut uniform. She made the doll a shirt he could wear when he visited earth occasionally. My gratitude and my joy grew. I made room in my life for the happy memory.

Maybe you're not like me and you're enjoying remembering a whole host of wonderful things about your own childhood, things you want to recreate for your child and you're looking forward to the rest of this journey.

Maybe you're experiencing a mix of emotions. Some of your childhood experiences may have been pleasant to recall while others are more painful to remember. In which case, you might be enjoying parts of this journey more than others.

You make sense to me. Take your time and do what you can. You got this!

Day 5: _____

If you could write a note to your younger self, what would it say?

Day 6: _____

My mother's greatest gift to me was ...

Day 7: _____

The lesson I'd like to bring from my relationship with my mother into my relationship with my child is …

Day 8: _____

Sometimes I'm like my dad. Sometimes I'm very different from my dad. The good thing about that is ...

Day 9: _____

The lesson I'd like to bring from my relationship with my dad into my relationship with my child is ...

I am not a simple sum of my parents and the experiences of my childhood. I am so much more. Yes, those things influenced my life and yet, I am more. How I respond, how I incorporate those experiences, the decisions I make about what my experiences mean to me, matter.

I am different than my parents. I am not my mother. I am not my father. I am not the step-mother who raised me. I am my own person. I parented differently than any of my parents did. I made my own decisions. Yes, I was impacted by the things they did right and the mistakes they made. I went on to make some of the same mistakes they did. And I made some new ones they never even thought of making.

I also did many things right that they never knew to do. I learned things they didn't know. I faced challenges they didn't, challenges all my own.

Thinking about how they impacted me gives me perspective. Looking at my choices and decisions, who I am and what I bring to my role as a mother is an important part of the journey.

This is a great place to apply grace. Be gentle with yourself. Every parent makes mistakes. Each parent brings something wonderful and amazing to the relationship. Press forward looking for the marvelousness that you bring, and you will find it. Acknowledge your imperfections. There's value in recognizing your vulnerabilities. Press on to discover and embrace your strengths. Build those and that's where you will find the courage, the motivation, the power to be the mother you truly desire to be for yourself and for your children.

You got this. I'm here for you.

The more you notice the good in yourself and your children, the lighter you'll feel. You'll find yourself happier, more playful, and more present for the good times. Goodbye overwhelm, negativity, and irritability. Hello patience and perspective.

You can do this!

Day 10: _____

Three things I like about myself as a mother are ...

Day 11: _____

When I feel like I've failed in the mom department, I feel comforted when I ...

Day 12: _____

I want to release these unrealistic demands I have for myself as a mom ...

We don't parent in a vacuum. We're impacted by those around us. The way we were parented, the way our parents were parented, all these things impact us.

Still, our children are born to us as separate people. They are uniquely their own persons. My son is neither me nor is he my husband. He was born his own person, right from the very start.

The person he is, what he brought with him into our relationship, has an impact on our mother-son relationship. I love that. Sometimes, I hated it too.

There were times when, if I could have controlled him, could have made him be who I wanted him to be, I would have tried. In hindsight I see it's good that wasn't something I could do.

I'm so glad my son is the unique person he is. I've learned so much from him. Not being in complete control of our relationship turned out to be a gift.

In the next section you'll look at who your child is and at what your child brings into your parent-child relationship.

Where you see a _____ in the prompt be sure to fill in your child's name. I recommend you focus on one child, even if you have several, as it's easier to be specific when you focus on your relationship with one child at a time. You can go back and answer the questions again, focusing on your relationship with each of your other children once you've completed this first set.

Tune in on how amazing your child is, and you'll enjoy being with your child more and more. Small changes in how you see your child, change how you approach that child. Seeing a child's marvelous and unique qualities make it easier to respond with empathy and patience. You'll lash out at your child less frequently. More empathy and patience will inspire appreciation in your child.

When gratitude comes back to me in the form of a kind word from my son, the revelation of something he learned from me that he finds valuable in his life now, my heart melts. I treasure those as gold.

Day 13: _____

A funny story I remember about _____ was when ...

Day 14: _____

The first moment I knew I loved _____ was when …

Day 15: _____

Something nice others say about my child is ...

Day 16: _____

Something my child does well is ...

Day 17: _____

I'm proud of my child when ...

Day 18: _____

Something my child does better than most kids I know is ...

Day 19: _____

One thing I believe my child will grow into that isn't coming easy right now is ...

Day 20: _____

When _____ feels discouraged, it helps if I ...

You've come half way in our journey together. This is a great time to sit a spell and take a little rest. Have a cup of coffee if you like!

I'm having a nice hot cup of my favorite mocha and thinking about a time when I was visiting with a friend and her daughter.

I was in Canada for a weeklong workshop. In the middle of the week, we had a day off to do some sight-seeing or shopping. I decided what I needed most was some time with my friend, Diane, and her two-year-old daughter, Miss B.

Diane suggested the best way to start our visit was at one of their favorite parks. The day was beautiful with loads of sunshine and a nice warm breeze. Miss B showed me around the park and I got to experience it all through her eyes.

Her wonder and delight at the ducks, her simple joy throwing sticks in the pond, the ease of following her lead as we wandered through the grass and around the water filled me with a sense of peace.

Her eyes sparkled as I listened and responded to what she was saying to me. I acknowledged her play with my words and she smiled with appreciation. I can't help but use the skills I teach in my program to connect with kids. They've become second nature to me. I felt refreshed in the joy of our connection. These are the moments I still treasure as I think back to that day.

Funny how a little time and a whole lot of closeness can fill a heart so full that even years later, the memory of it can bring a rush of happiness. Taking the time to recall and appreciate the good, to be grateful for the challenges and lessons learned, these are the things that strengthen me to continue growing. Because I take the time to be grateful, I can connect on a deeper level. I see myself and others around me in a new, more positive light.

Thanks for coming this far with me. There's more good things up the road. You'll see!

Day 21: _____

My favorite snuggle time with _____ is/was?

Day 22: _____

Though _____ is past the age for cuddles, we still enjoy affection by ...

Day 23: _____

My child surprised me with something unexpectedly delightful when ...

Day 24: _____

If I could relive one moment with my child, it would be when ...

Day 25: _____

Some good things about my child might be easy for me to miss if I didn't stop and think carefully about it. Three good things about my child that might normally fall under my radar are ...

Day 26: _____

I feel closest to _____ when we ...

As I watched Darcy trying to contain her excitement about her first time in the playroom with me, I thought about how I've been too excited to express my overwhelming emotion and do the thing I came to do. I remember feeling like that. The restless enthusiasm was so big that I had no idea how to take hold of the experience and jump into action.

Her joy stirred my own. I came into the play session excited about a recent discovery that had me feeling overjoyed. Seeing Darcy's joy touched a chord in me. I was with her when she exclaimed, "I am so freaking excited." Sometimes kids have a way of unleashing something in me that I couldn't quite get a handle on earlier. It was like that with Darcy. I was looking in a mirror and seeing my own heart.

Darcy finally found her mojo. She metaphorically dipped her feet into the water and before you know it, she was swimming like a pro. And really, it didn't take her that long. By the time our play session was over, she looked and sounded like any other fully involved play therapy adventurer. She was using her imagination and pretending, taking on daring roles and trying out new things.

Brené Brown defines connection as "the energy between people when they feel seen, heard, and valued … when they are strengthened by the relationship."

Before our playtime was up, Darcy was sharing stories and secrets with me. I felt connected. I knew she felt the connection too because when our time was over, she expressed regret at leaving. We talked about how much we were looking forward to her next powerful playtime.

I'm grateful for the connections that have inspired me to reach out courageously for closeness and relationship. Gratitude is a tool that brings out the best in us. Gratitude draws you and your child closer. Great parenting doesn't require perfection. It demands connection. Your warm connection endures and creates a powerful legacy.

Do you remember playing as a kid? Who connected with you in your playtimes?

Day 27: _____

The qualities I hope to see blossom as my child grows are ...

Day 28: _____

For my child's future, I am believing …

Day 29: _____

To support my hope for my child, I am …

Day 30: _____

If I could only give my child one thing, I would want to give him/her ...

We are coming to the last section. How's it going?

It's time to reflect on where you've come so far, review what you've discovered and record what you want to take into the future with you because motherhood truly is a process of growth not only for kids but for moms too!

Alicia Keyes said, "Being a parent has made me more open, more connected to myself, more happy and a better person all the way around."

In this last section you'll have the opportunity to explore how you and your child are supporting and encouraging one another to grow as you journey through motherhood.

I'd love to hear about what you've been discovering as you have been exploring your thoughts and feelings about motherhood. Come on over to my Facebook group: *Play Connect Influence* and share something you like about yourself as a mother. You'll find the group at: https://www.facebook.com/groups/playconnect/

The weight of psychological research says that gratitude reduces the effects of stress and improves happiness, vitality, and life satisfaction. Gratitude promotes feelings of connectedness and an increased depth of understanding between mothers and their children. Because of this you're likely feeling closer to your child. You may be feeling an increased sense of support, particularly if you've been participating in the Facebook group.

Motherhood may not be all blue skies and butterflies but there's a good likelihood that by this point in our journey you're beginning to feel grateful for the good times. You may even be feeling grateful for the stormy weather that you've experienced as you hiked this trail.

I want you to know, I'm here to cheer you on, to bear witness of your courage on the trip, and to guide you onward. You're making amazing progress. You're just 10 days from the end of this 40-day trek.

Day 31: _____

Something my child has taught me is ...

Day 32: _____

I wish I was more ...

Day 33: _____

I wish I was less ...

Day 34: _____

I wish my child was more ...

Day 35: _____

I wish my child was less …

Day 36: _____

I am glad I am ...

Day 37: _____

I am glad my child is ...

Day 38: _____

While life with my child is far from perfect, one thing I'm grateful for about my child is ...

Day 39: _____

My child challenges me to be my very best self when ...

Day 40: _____

Being a mom to _____ is worth the struggle when ...

Congratulations! You made it to the end of this part of your journey. Thank you for celebrating your journey through motherhood with me here and in the Facebook group, *Play Connect Influence*. You'll find the group at: https://www.facebook.com/groups/playconnect/   I hope that this is just the beginning of your celebration as you continue to discover more to like about yourself as a mom.

I hope we can continue the conversation about kids, the challenges, and the delights of motherhood. If we were having this conversation at our favorite lunch spot, we'd be talking about many things. Things like the things your mom did so nicely that you'd like to make sure you do those for your own kids. Things like the mistakes she made that you don't ever want to repeat. Things like how hard it is and how sweet it is to watch your kids grow up and become more independent.

We'd talk about your hopes and dreams for your relationship with your kids and see your dreams expand beyond the daily grind to a place where love flourishes beautifully, even as your children become adults. You might be like the mom who told me that she didn't know it was possible for her teenage son to care about her feelings, to notice and offer to help her. She admitted that when he did, it surprised her. She felt supported and loved and that those were good feelings she wanted more of in her relationship with him.

I'd share with you the things that encouraged me along the way and listen to the things I wish never happened to you. Eventually, we'd get to the part of the conversation where we'd talk about what's next.

Come to think of it, let's head there now. Let's have that conversation because isn't that really what we're doing here. The next step is here: http://www.playtimewisdom.com/courageousnextstep/

You've worked courageously in our time together. You inspired me to create a few more writing prompts to help you envision the relationship you'd like to have with your children as adults. This is a good time in our conversation to dream about what you're creating with your child for the future. I want to give you some bonus writing prompts to guide you in imagining the sweet possibilities for you and your child.

It seems so far away now but you're moving quickly towards a time when your child will be fully grown and independent.

You're a mom. That's your big goal: a happy, successful, independent adult who in your heart will always be your precious child.

You've explored your relationship with your parents and discovered a few things you'd like to keep and treasure. You may have even discovered a few things you want to discard and move past. You've discovered some things you like about yourself as a mom and some things you're grateful for in your child. You've explored some areas where you would like to see your child grow and some areas where you'd like to grow as a mom.

You're noticing the good things about being a mom more often than you were before you began this journey. You're noticing things you're grateful for about your child and feeling encouraged. You're hoping to keep that going and realizing that keeping the momentum will be challenging.

Exploring your hopes and dreams for your adult relationship with your child will give you a sense of excitement and adventure as your children age. Your child will grow up and you will have a relationship of some kind. Even a conflicted or estranged relationship is a relationship. We never stop being a mom no matter how old our kids get. Spending time exploring your desires will shine a light on the path towards the future relationship you want.

This courageous next step will empower you to maintain the momentum and energy you've gained as you found a new courageously grateful perspective of your child and of yourself as a mother. I'm grateful that we shared this part of your hike. I look forward to the next leg of our journey together.

Come join me at: http://www.playtimewisdom.com/courageousnextstep/

I'll meet you there.

A HEARTFELT THANK YOU TO...

David Woods who partnered with me in parenting every step of the way,

Ryan Woods who lived the experiment and has survived to flourish beautifully,

Rebecca Woods, whose presence brings me incredible joy,

My mommy, Patricia Pearl, whose heart can never be untangled from mine,

My daddy, Wayne, who met and married the sweetest mommy and raised me without her when schizophrenia took her from us, whose eyes never failed to sparkle in my presence.

Virginia Muzquiz, first my friend and then my first raving fan, who bravely played in the sculpture park with me.

Karin Olson, who keeps insisting the world needs my brand of genius,

Dr. Margaret Robling, whose quirky, stable, and gentle spirit has contributed more than anyone will ever know,

Kayla Olson, Jenn Duehring, Gary Scott, Marilyn Pride, Terry-Lynn Aplin, Elijah and Ben Olson whose support enabled me to do this book.

Callan Rush, whose connection to an audience inspires me to connect more boldly,

Gitte Lassen, Joan Brooks, and Erin Bentley, who kept me accountable to get it done.

Una Archer who has inspired me with her tender approach to mothering.

Paul Keetch, who walked me step by step through creating my online program, Playtime Power!

Jennifer Ross Mazella, who helps moms of kids with special needs navigate through the educational system,

My Cave Springs Toastmasters, whose feedback and encouragement has grown my heart a few sizes bigger.

Each of the photographers who provided the lovely photos that make this book more beautiful.

Drs. Mike and Nancy Smith, PhDs who shared their work and their hearts,

Diane Rolston, who supported me in my journey through frustration and her Miss B who played with me when I needed refreshing.

Dr. Tony Victor who helped me to clarify my thoughts and feelings and, in whose presence, connection happens,

Leona Bicknese and my Voelkerding Village family, who allowed me to share their lives and hold their babies,

St. Louis Mamas and West County Moms who supported me in making important editorial decisions.

Kate Brockmeyer whose forward thinking brought into existence the only professional photos of me and my mommy.

Child psychologist, Dr. Bob Agnew who first nurtured my belief in my capacity to heal myself and others,

Joel S. Levinson, who walked with me through my mommy's final days with compassion and cheered me on in the days that followed.

Jeff Steele who challenged me to write a book instead of trying to write a book. Thanks Jeff! I did it!

Kaye Putnam and Sarah Putnam, who have supported me in bringing my brand to life.

Dr. Shari Miller, Jami Midcap Kirkbride and my Brand New Brand family who came alongside me with feedback and support through many revisions.

Beth Appelbaum Bachman, who handed out a ton of hand-outs at my live event and still stuck around to be my friend.

Barbara, who married my daddy and gave me a home, stood in for my mommy, sewed doll clothes for my dolls, and taught me to embroider just like my own mommy would have if she had been able.

Don Lebaige and Rosanne Thomas Lebaige, who show up for me.

Timothy Wayne, who cherished our childhood together and remembered the good for me.

And God who gave me all these beautiful people and more to love, help and support me.

MEET YOUR TOUR GUIDE

"I look forward to the day when there's no longer a need for child therapists in the world. Until then, I'm going to keep bringing smiles and laughter to as many moms and kids as possible."

Deborah Woods, NCC, equips moms to raise happy kids, with great people skills, who grow up to be successful happy adults.

"Because the parent-child relationship is the best place for a child to grow, I created the Playtime Power Program to help moms gain access to the wellspring of privileged information I discovered in my play therapy training. I'm excited that in the comfort of their own homes, parents are equipped to unleash joyful connection with their kids in just 30 minutes a week."

"I'm committed to helping moms and kids get the help that wasn't available to my family when we first needed it. Although the approach had been around in academic circles, it wasn't being shared widely enough to get to us. I am changing that."

Over the years, Deborah's expertise has been honored with a Master of Arts degree in Psychological Counseling, a board certification of National Certified Counselor and State of Missouri License in Professional Counseling. Deborah has spent over 15,000 hours playing with kids.

Deborah enjoys playing Guild Wars with her son and his friends, visiting Laumeier Sculpture Park with family and friends, spending time watching Star Trek and John Wayne movies with her husband, attorney, David Woods, and making time for a strategic game of Settlers of Catan with longtime friends.